RUBANK EDUCATIONAL LIBRARY No. 59

Soloist Folio

FOR

B♭ CORNET OR TRUMPET (BARITONE 𝄞)

with Piano Accompaniment

CONTENTS

		Solo Part	Piano Part
ACHILLES	R. M. Endresen	14	30
ADESTE FIDELIS (O Come, All Ye Faithful)	Reading-Davis	24	54
CARNIVAL OF VENICE Air Varie	Henry W. Davis	4	8
EL CAPITAN Valse Caprice	Geo. E. Worth	18	40
FRIENDS Waltz Caprice	Clay Smith	2	2
GLEN EDEN Polka	Chas. W. Storm	6	14
HEROICA	E. DeLamater	3	6
LE SECRET Intermezzo	Gautier-Davis	12	27
MIRAGE, THE Mazurka Capriccioso	George H. Tyler	16	35
MOCKING BIRD Fantasia	Hawthorne-Johnson	22	48
MY BUDDY POLKA	Ervin Kleffman	8	18
NEW FRIENDSHIP Concert Polka	Chas. W. Storm	10	22
O COME, ALL YE FAITHFUL (Adeste Fidelis)	Reading-Davis	24	54
SIRIUS	VanderCook	20	44

RUBANK®

HAL•LEONARD® CORPORATION

7777 W. BLUEMOUND RD. P.O. BOX 13819 MILWAUKEE, WI 53213

Dedicated to all my friends

FRIENDS

WALTZ CAPRICE

CLAY SMITH

Brightly
f
dolce
p
dolce
p

Tempo I
f
mf
mf
rit.
a tempo
rit.
a tempo
rit.
a tempo
rit.
a tempo

rit.
a tempo
rit.
a tempo
Vivo
f
Vivo
f
cresc.
cresc.

HEROICA

E. DeLAMATER

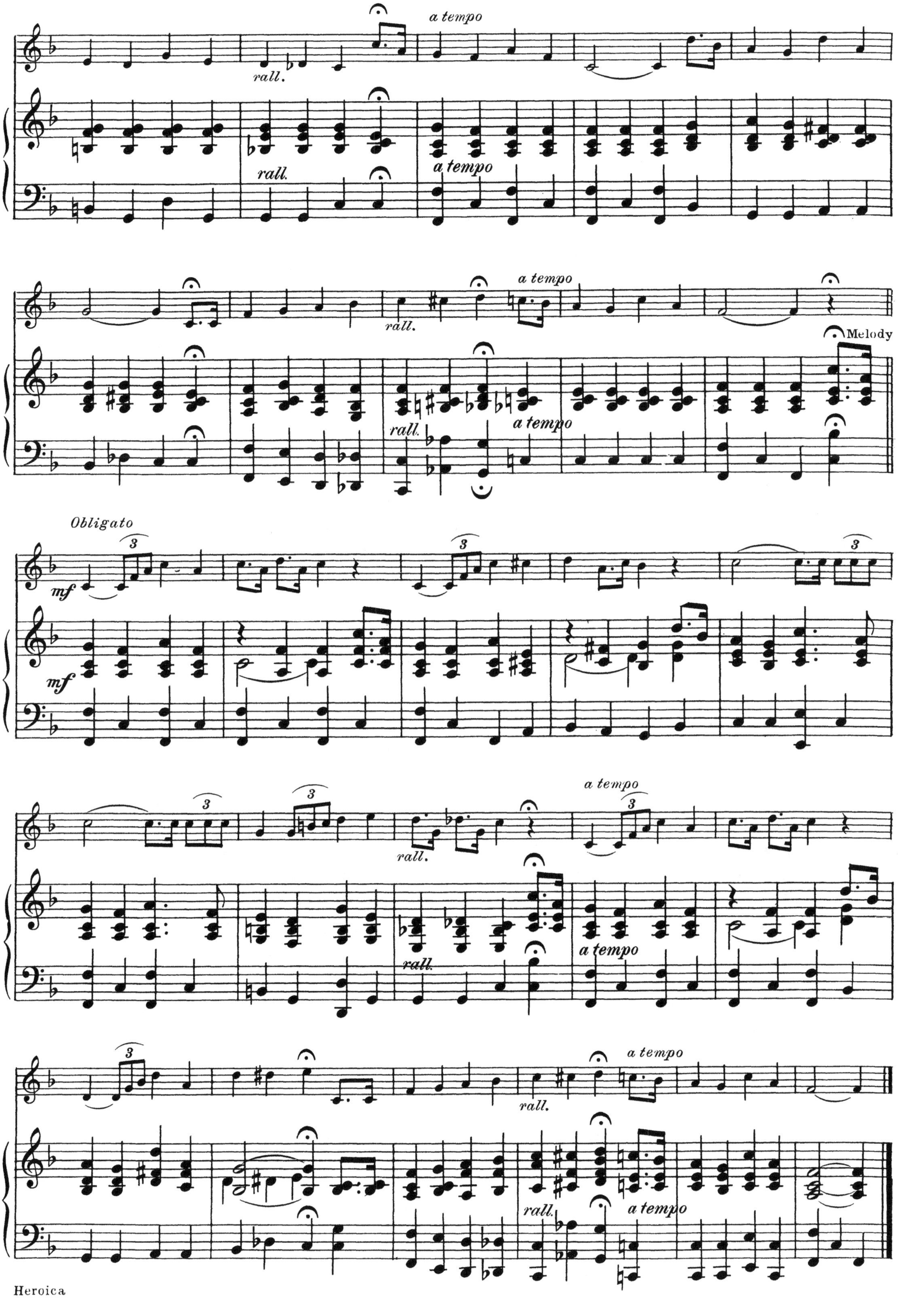
a tempo
rall.
rall.
a tempo
a tempo
rall.
rall.
a tempo
Melody
Obligato
mf
mf
a tempo
rall.
rall.
a tempo
a tempo
rall.
rall.
a tempo

Carnival of Venice

Air Varie

Piano

HENRY W. DAVIS

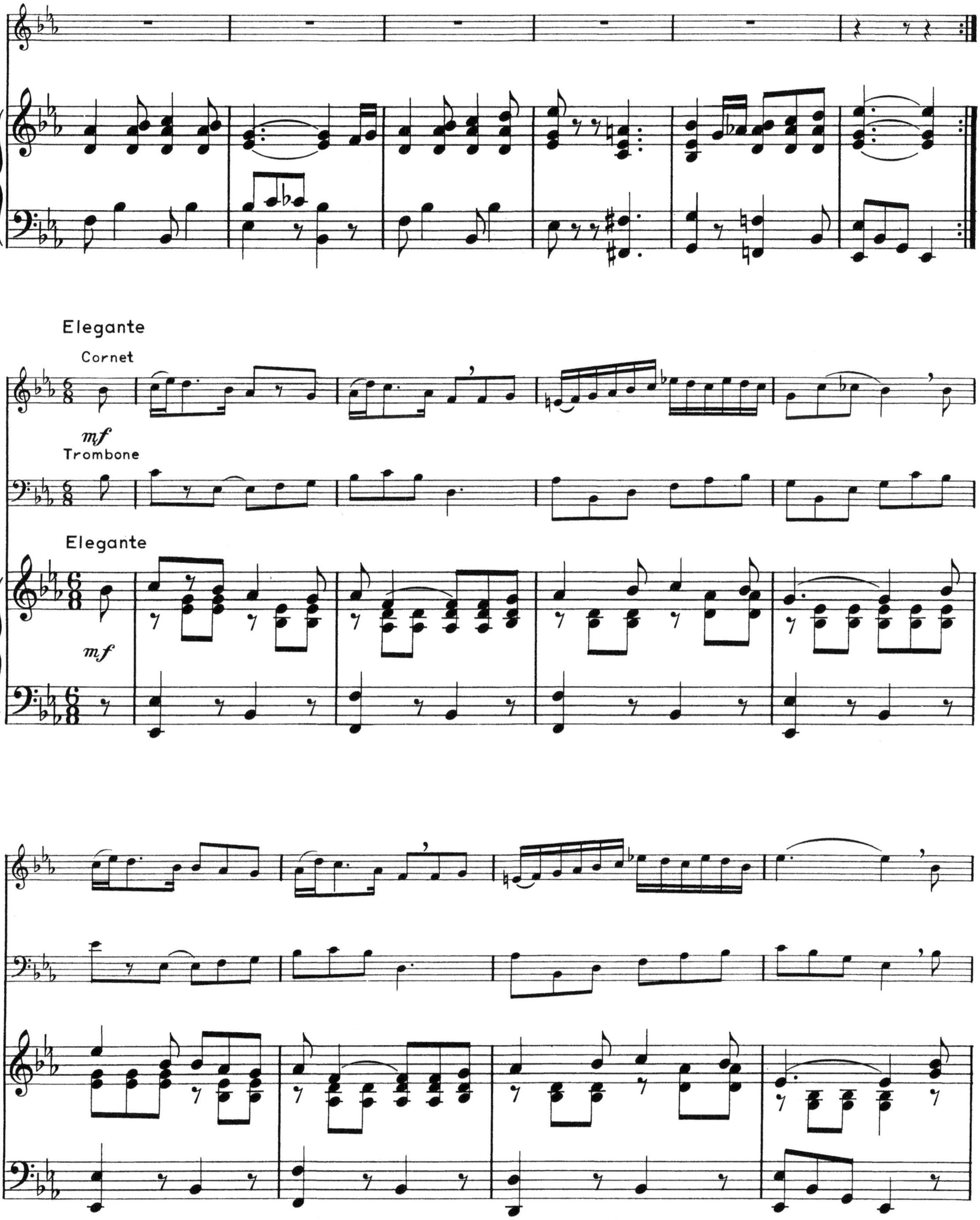
Elegante
Cornet
mf
Trombone
Elegante
mf

Animato
f

Gran gusto
mf
Gran gusto
mf

Animato
f
mf
Cad.
Con grazia
mf
mf
mf

accel.
accel.
f
marcato
f
rit.

GLEN EDEN
POLKA

Piano

CHAS. W. STORM

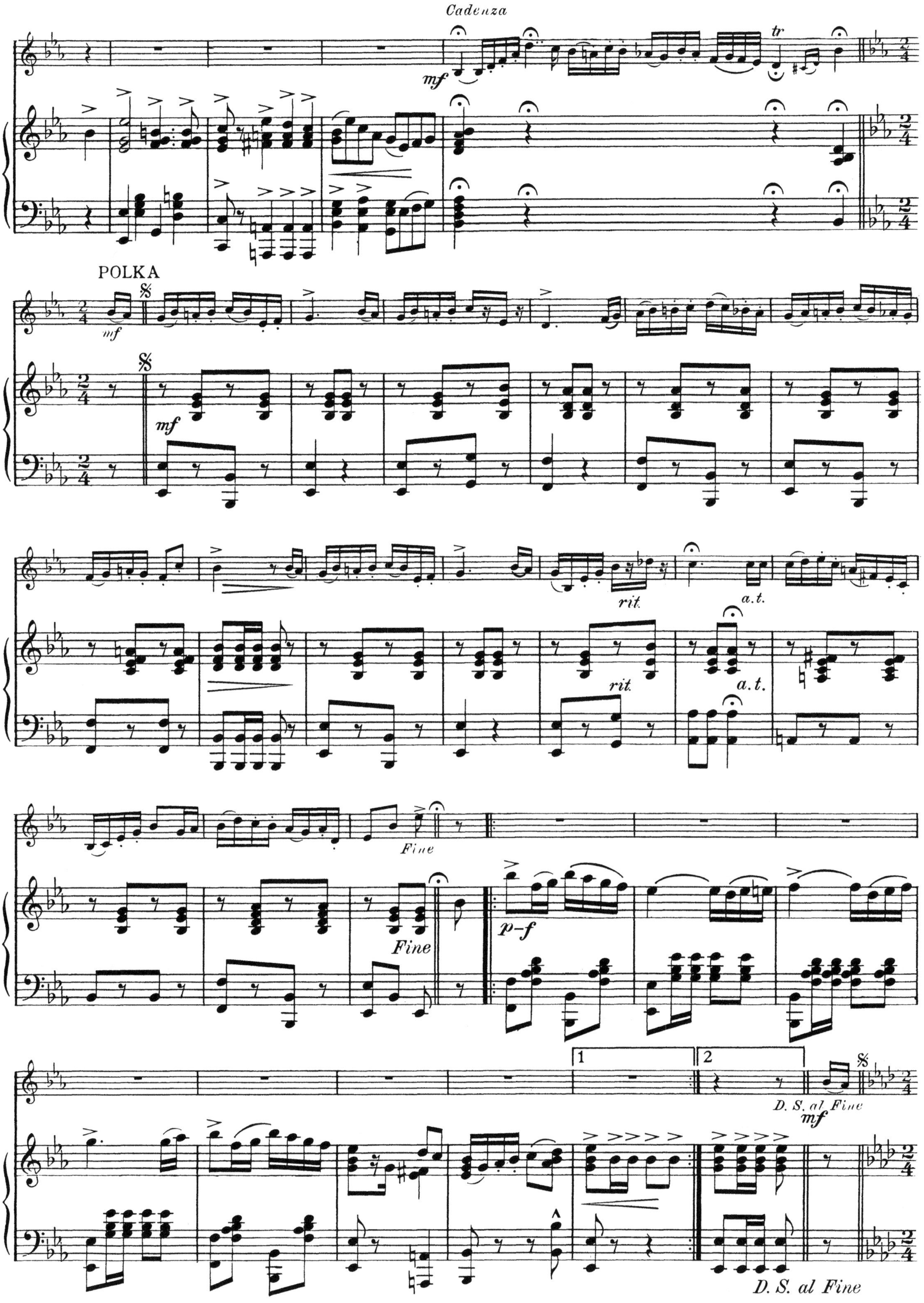
Cadenza
mf
tr
POLKA
mf
rit.
a.t.
Fine
p-f
1
2
D. S. al Fine

TRIO
Slow dolce
Moderato
p-f
ff
p
rit.
a tempo
rit.
a tempo
POLKA
ff

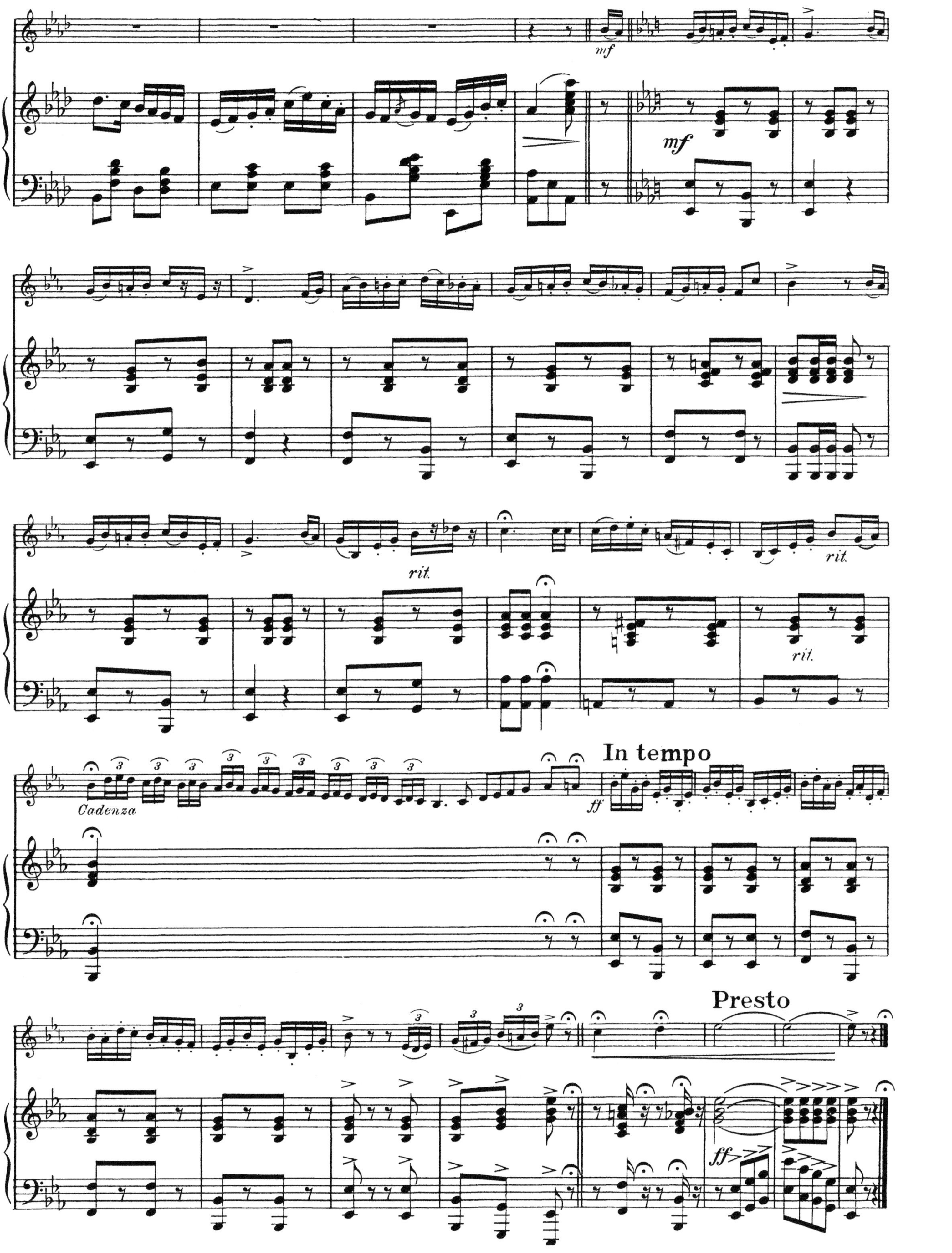
mf
mf
rit.
rit.
rit.
Cadenza
In tempo
ff
Presto
ff

MY BUDDY POLKA

ERVIN KLEFFMAN

1
2
f
Polka Not too fast
mf
Polka
mf

TRIO
a little slower
mf
a little slower
mf
accel.
accel.
Fast
Tutti
ff
1
2
f

Polka *Not too fast*
mf
Polka
mf
CODA
f accel.
f poco a poco
ff

NEW FRIENDSHIP

Concert Polka

CHAS. W. STORM

Tempo I
rit.
rit.
f
rall.
Polka
Solo
mf
mf
f
rit.
a tempo
rit.
a tempo

Fine
Fine
f
1
2
Solo
D.S. al Fine
D.S. al Fnie
TRIO
Solo Slower
p
ff
rit.
p-f

POLKA
ff

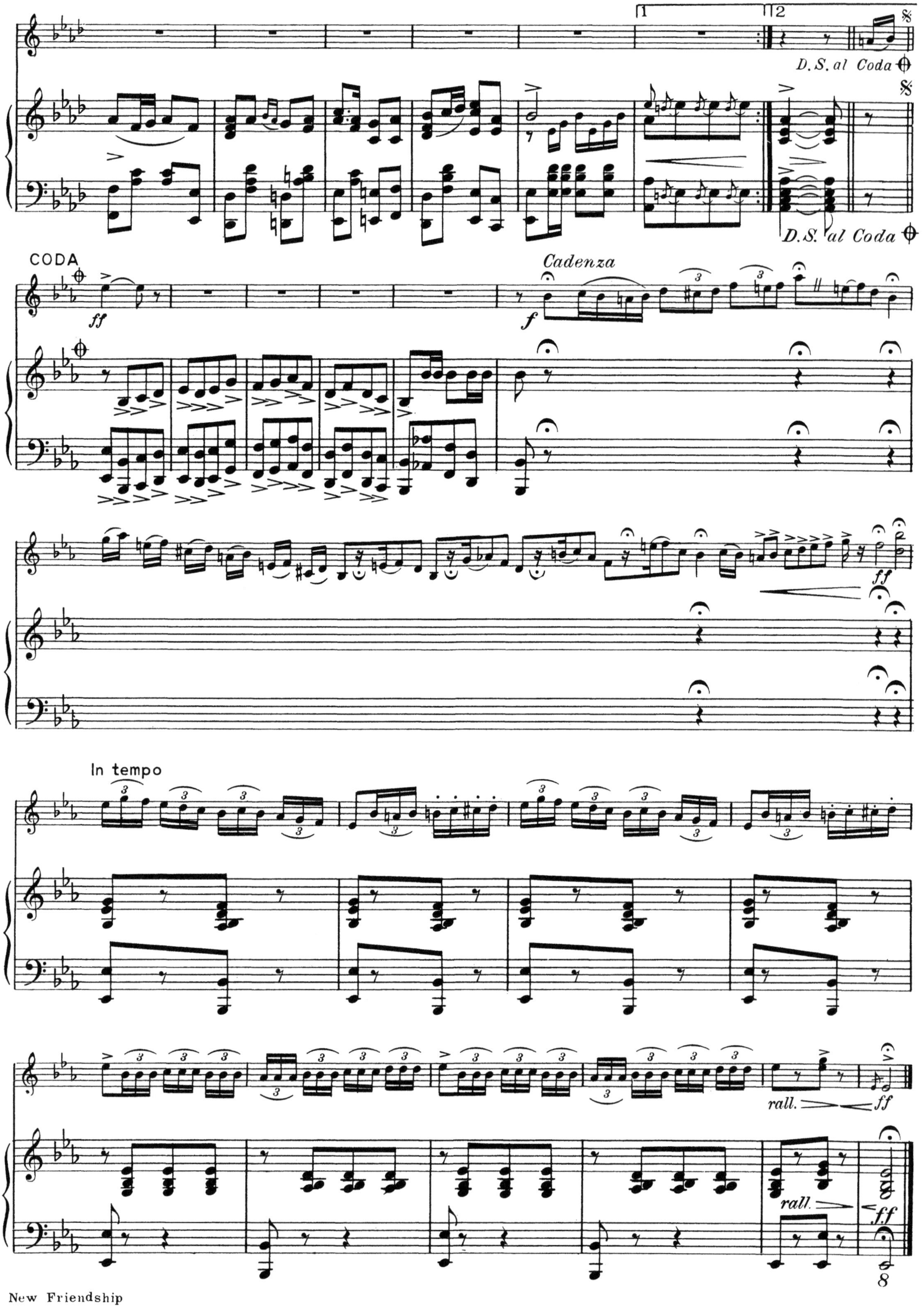
1
2
D.S. al Coda
D.S. al Coda
CODA
Cadenza
ff
f
ff
In tempo
rall.
ff
rall.
ff
8

Le Secret

INTERMEZZO

PIANO ACCOMP.

LEONARD GAUTIER
Arr. by Henry W. Davis

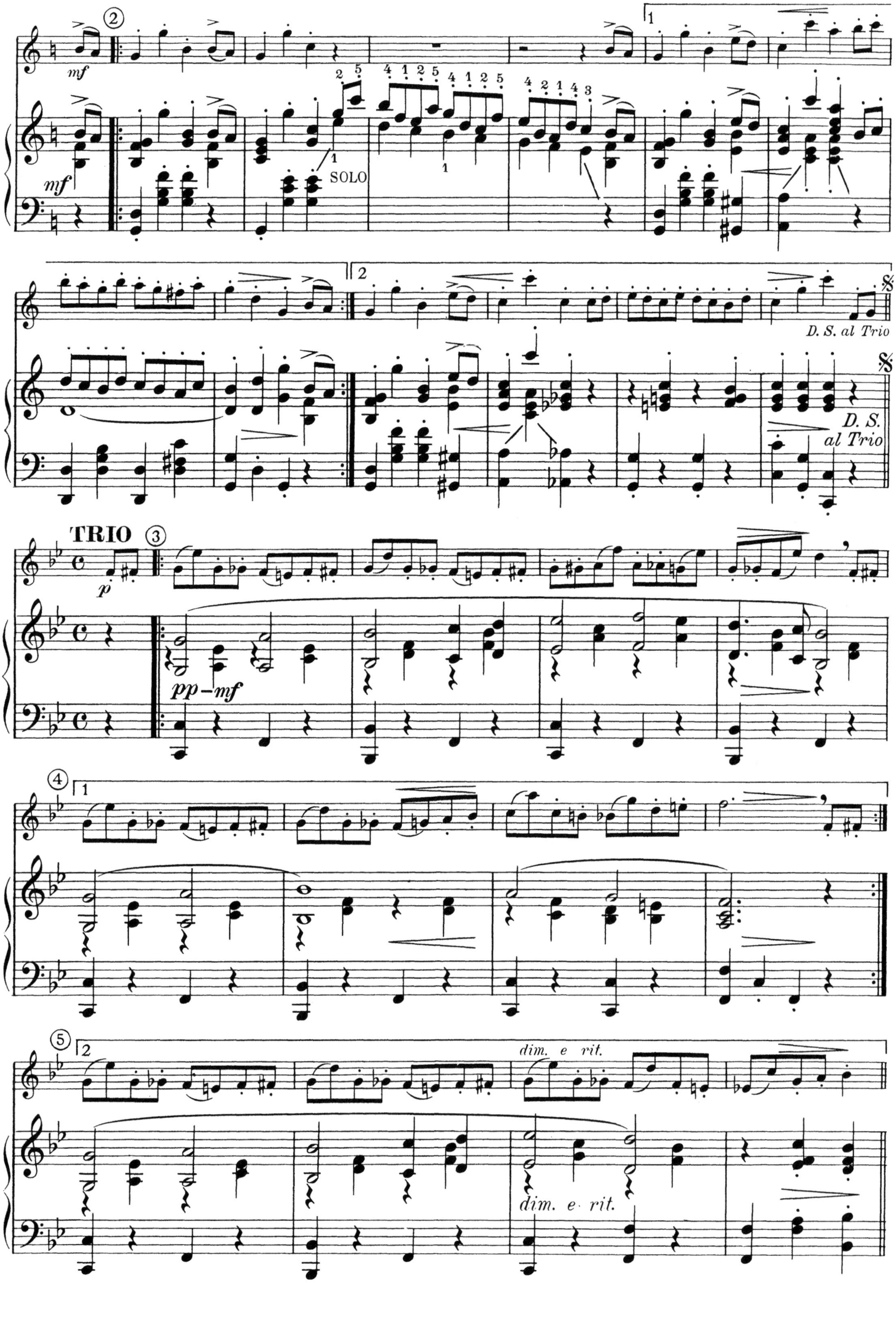
2
mf
SOLO
D. S. al Trio
D. S. al Trio
TRIO
3
p
pp–mf
4
5
dim. e rit.
dim. e rit.

RUBANK EDUCATIONAL LIBRARY No. 59

Soloist Folio

FOR

B♭ CORNET OR TRUMPET (BARITONE 𝄞)

with Piano Accompaniment

CONTENTS

		Solo Part	Piano Part
ACHILLES	R. M. Endresen	14	30
ADESTE FIDELIS (O Come, All Ye Faithful)	Reading-Davis	24	54
CARNIVAL OF VENICE Air Varie	Henry W. Davis	4	8
EL CAPITAN Valse Caprice	Geo. E. Worth	18	40
FRIENDS Waltz Caprice	Clay Smith	2	2
GLEN EDEN Polka	Chas. W. Storm	6	14
HEROICA	E. DeLamater	3	6
LE SECRET Intermezzo	Gautier-Davis	12	27
MIRAGE, THE Mazurka Capriccioso	George H. Tyler	16	35
MOCKING BIRD Fantasia	Hawthorne-Johnson	22	48
MY BUDDY POLKA	Ervin Kleffman	8	18
NEW FRIENDSHIP Concert Polka	Chas. W. Storm	10	22
O COME, ALL YE FAITHFUL (Adeste Fidelis)	Reading-Davis	24	54
SIRIUS	VanderCook	20	44

RUBANK®

HAL•LEONARD® CORPORATION
7777 W. BLUEMOUND RD. P.O. BOX 13819 MILWAUKEE, WI 53213

Dedicated to all my friends

FRIENDS

B♭ Cornet or Trumpet

WALTZ CAPRICE

CLAY SMITH

Also published with Band accompaniment.

HEROICA

B♭ Cornet

E. DeLAMATER

Also published for Trombone or Baritone Bass Clef

Carnival of Venice

Air Varie

B♭ Cornet or Trumpet

HENRY W. DAVIS

B♭ Cornet or Trumpet

GLEN EDEN
POLKA

Solo B♭ Cornet or Trumpet

Baritone 𝄞

Range 

CHAS. W. STORM

This Solo is also published for Baritone and Trombone in Bass Clef.

Solo B♭ Cornet or Trumpet

MY BUDDY POLKA

Solo Cornet I

ERVIN KLEFFMAN

Also published for Band in same key.

Solo Cornet I

NOTE: All sixteenth notes in this composition should be played with an extremely Legato Style of tonguing--most of the eighth notes are marked staccato.

Range 

NEW FRIENDSHIP

Time of Performance 5 min.

B♭ Trumpet

Cornet-Baritone 𝄞

Concert Polka

CHAS. W. STORM

TRIO
Tutti
rit.
Solo Slower
Polka
Tutti
Solo
D. S. al Coda
Tutti
Cadenza
In tempo
rall

Le Secret

INTERMEZZO

B♭ CORNET SOLO

LEONARD GAUTIER
Arr. by Henry W. Davis

B♭ Cornet Solo

Range 

Time of Performance 3 min.

ACHILLES

Solo B♭ Cornet or Trumpet

Trombone or Baritone 𝄞

R. M. ENDRESEN

Solo B♭ Cornet or Trumpet

The Mirage

Mazurka Capriccioso

Solo B♭ Cornet
or Trumpet

GEORGE H. TYLER

a piacere
mf
molto accel. e cresc.
f
mf
a tempo
rall.
ff
p
poco accel.
1
2
rit.
mf
6
Allegro vivace
TUTTI
14
Solo
tempo rubato
mf
rubato
accel.
rit.
a tempo
rubato
accel.
accel.
Coda animato
f
Lento
Presto
4
7
accel.
ff

El Capitan

Valse Caprice

Solo for Cornet or Trumpet

Cornet or Trumpet
(Baritone 𝄞)

GEO. E. WORTH

Cornet or Trumpet

SIRIUS

9

Progressive Etudes for Cornet or Trumpet

VANDER COOK

accel.
rit.
16
TRIO
brilliante
mp
mf
rit.
f
slowly
mf
accel.
15
1
Moderato
mf
rit.
a tempo
mf
rit.
f
slowly
p
Cadenza
Vivace
f

Mocking Bird

FANTASIA

Cornet Solo

Cornet Solo

ALICE HAWTHORNE
Transcribed by Clair W. Johnson

23

Cornet Solo

Adeste Fideles

(O Come, All Ye Faithful)

Solo B♭ Cornet
or Trumpet

JOHN READING
Arr. by Henry W. Davis

6
f a tempo
a tempo
cresc.
cresc
7
pp
pp—mf
8
1
9
2
dim.
D.S. al Coda
D. S. al Coda
10
CODA
p
dim.
pp rall.
ppp
f
8va

ACHILLES

Solo for Cornet, Trombone or Baritone

R. M. ENDRESEN

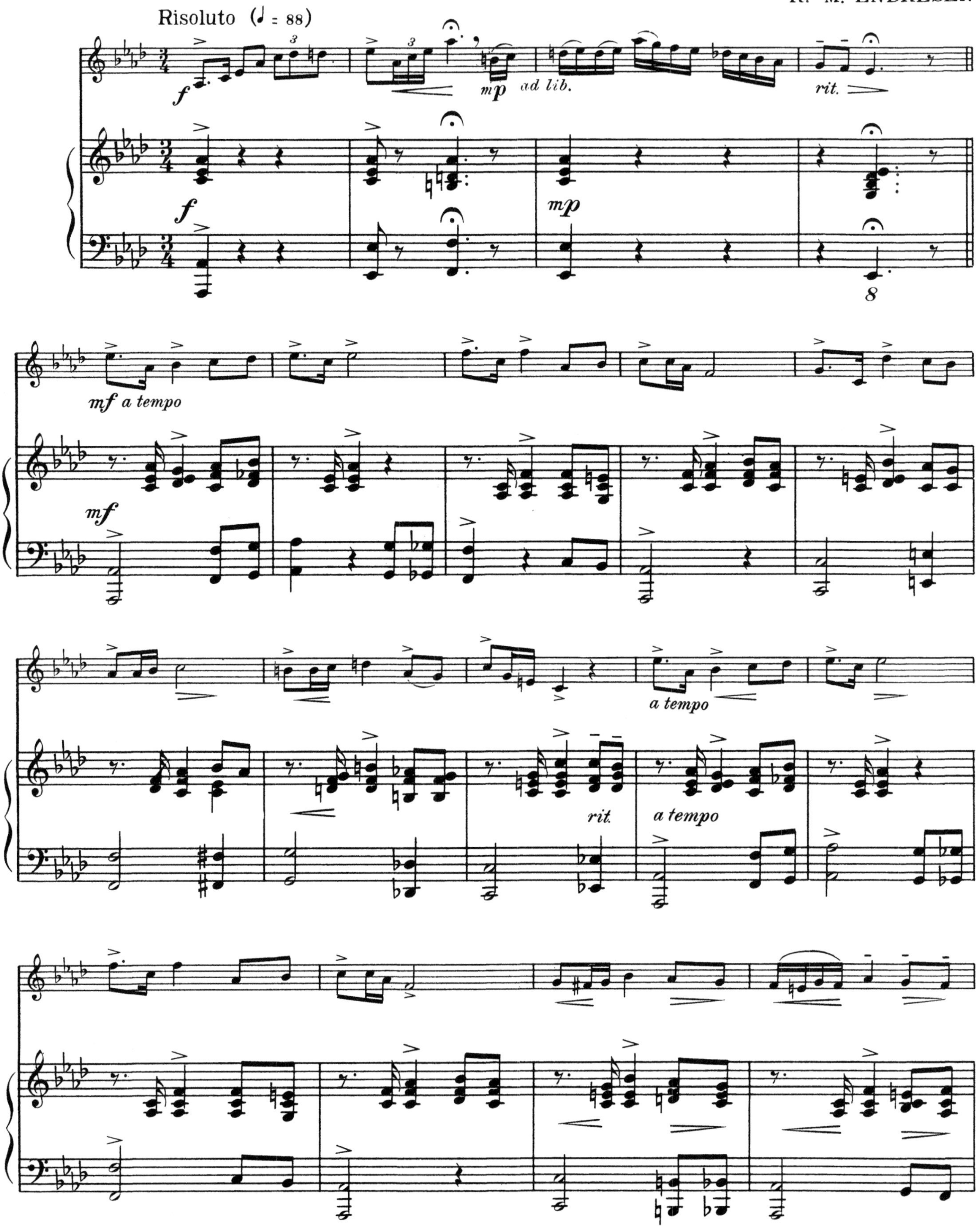

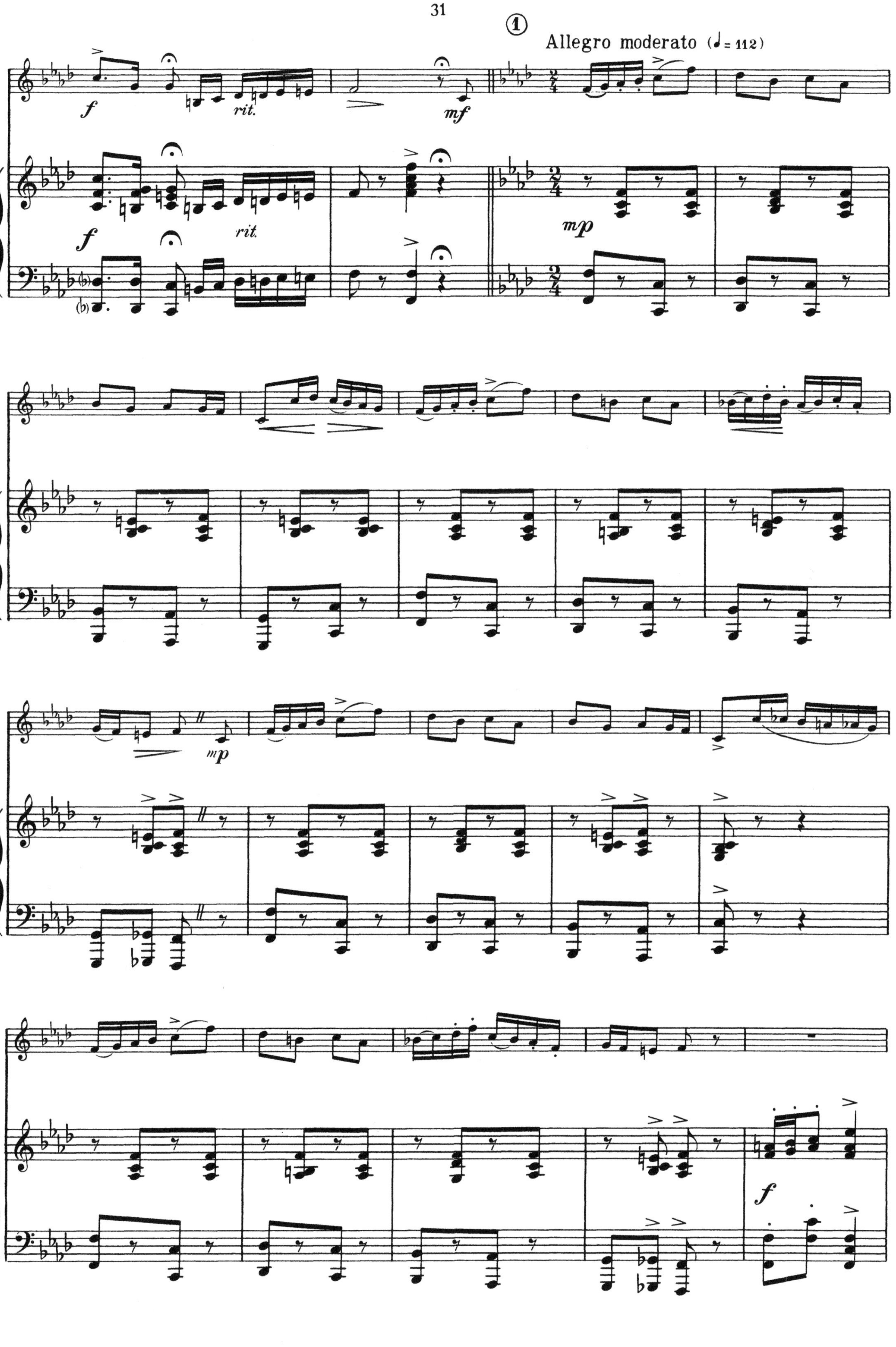
1
Allegro moderato (♩= 112)
f
rit.
mf
f
rit.
mp
mp
f

2
mf
mp
f
mp
f
mf
rit.
3
p espressivo
p
vivace
vivace
mf

1
2
4
mf
espressivo
mf
3
3
vivace
mf
mp
vivace
f
accel.
ad lib.
f

5
Tempo I
R.H.
L.H.
R.H.
3
3
L.H.
R
L
3
mf
a tempo
a tempo
rit.
rit.
rit.
6
f a tempo
f a tempo
allargando
f
f allargando

The Mirage

Mazurka Capriccioso

Piano

GEORGE H. TYLER

tempo rubato
rubato
mf
accel.
rit.
a tempo
accel.
a tempo
f
Allegro
ffz
p
rall.
D.S. al

Maestoso
rit.
a piacere
molto accel. e cresc.
a tempo
rall.
molto accel. e
cresc.
a tempo

ff
p poco accel.
p poco accel.
1
rit.
mf
2
Allegro vivace
rit.
fz
ffz
ff
Solo
mf

tempo rubato
rubato
mf
accel.
rit.
a tempo
CODA Animato
f
Lento
Presto
ff
ffz

El Capitan

Piano

Valse Caprice

Solo for Cornet or Trumpet

GEO. E. WORTH

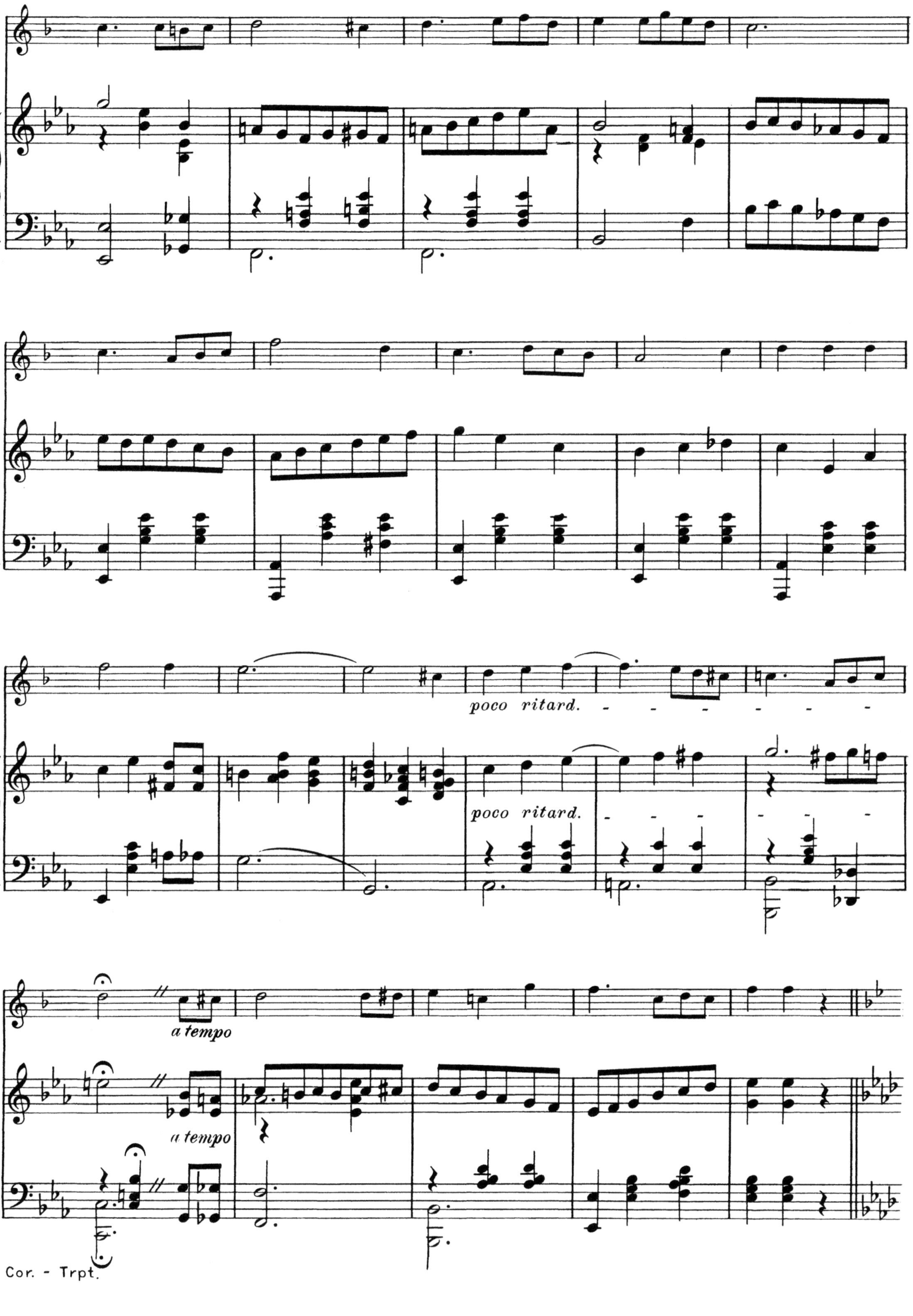
poco ritard.
poco ritard.
a tempo
a tempo

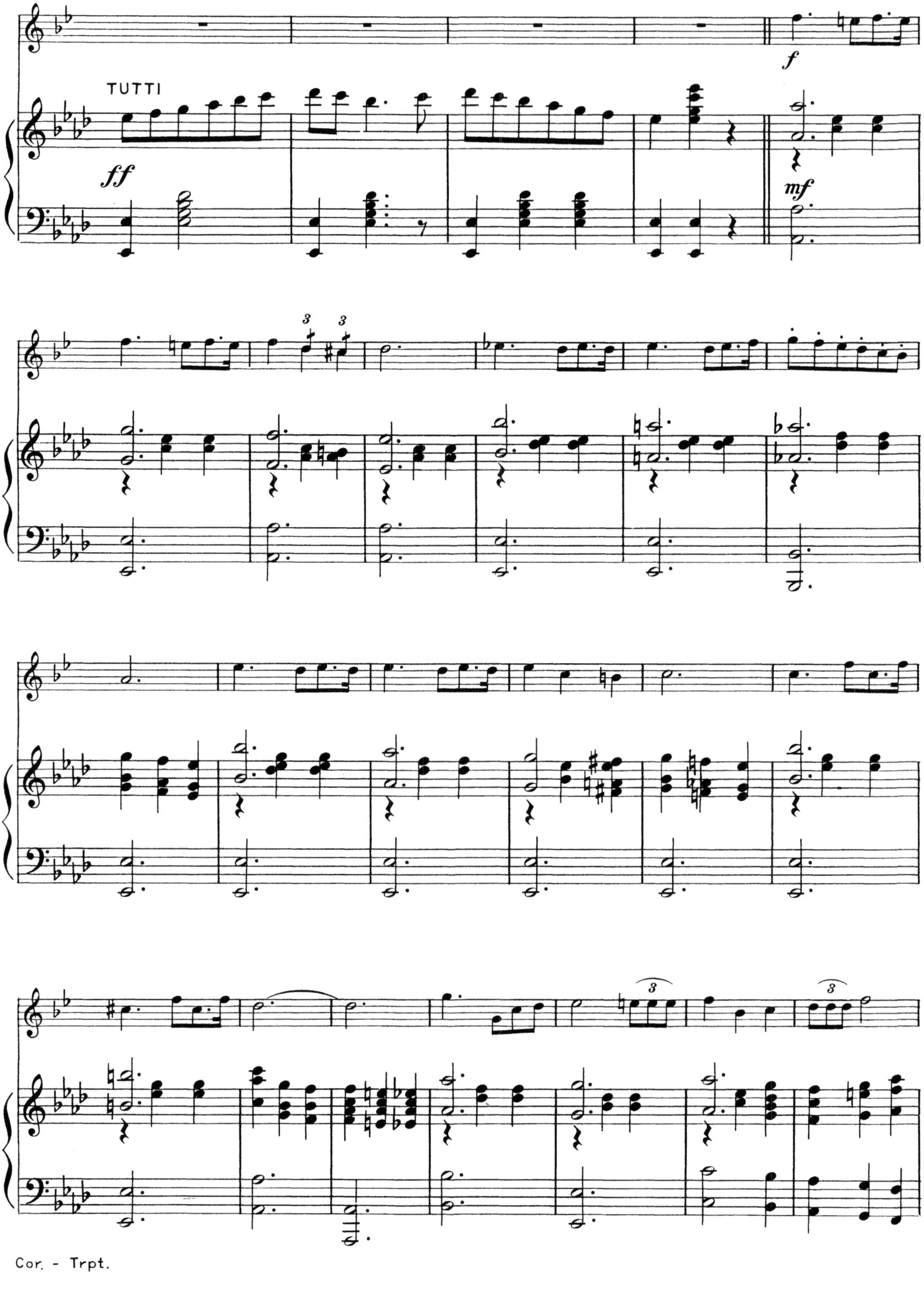
TUTTI
ff
f
mf
3
3
3
3

accel.
accel.
ff
ff
Allegro
Optional
ff
ff

SIRIUS

9

Progressive Etudes for Cornet or Trumpet

VANDER COOK

Pesante
rit.
p rit.
Moderato
Moderato
rit.
rit.
a tempo
mf a tempo
rit.
slowly
slowly
accel.
accel.

rit.
rit.
f
1
2
TRIO
brilliante
mp
mf
TRIO
mp
mf
mp
rit.
f
mp
rit.
f

slowly
mf
accel.
slowly
mf
accel.
f
1
2
D. S.
CODA
Cadenza
Vivace
f
CODA
Cadenza
Vivace
f

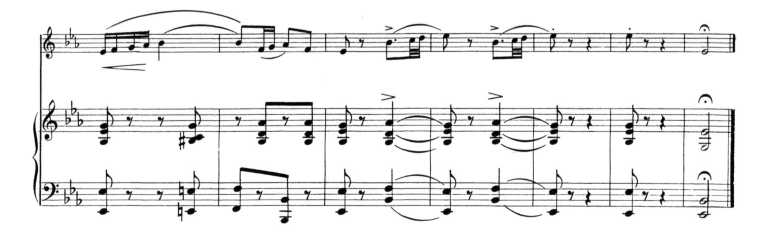

Mocking Bird

FANTASIA

Cornet Solo

ALICE HAWTHORNE
Transcribed by Clair W. Johnson

mf
p
fluently
p

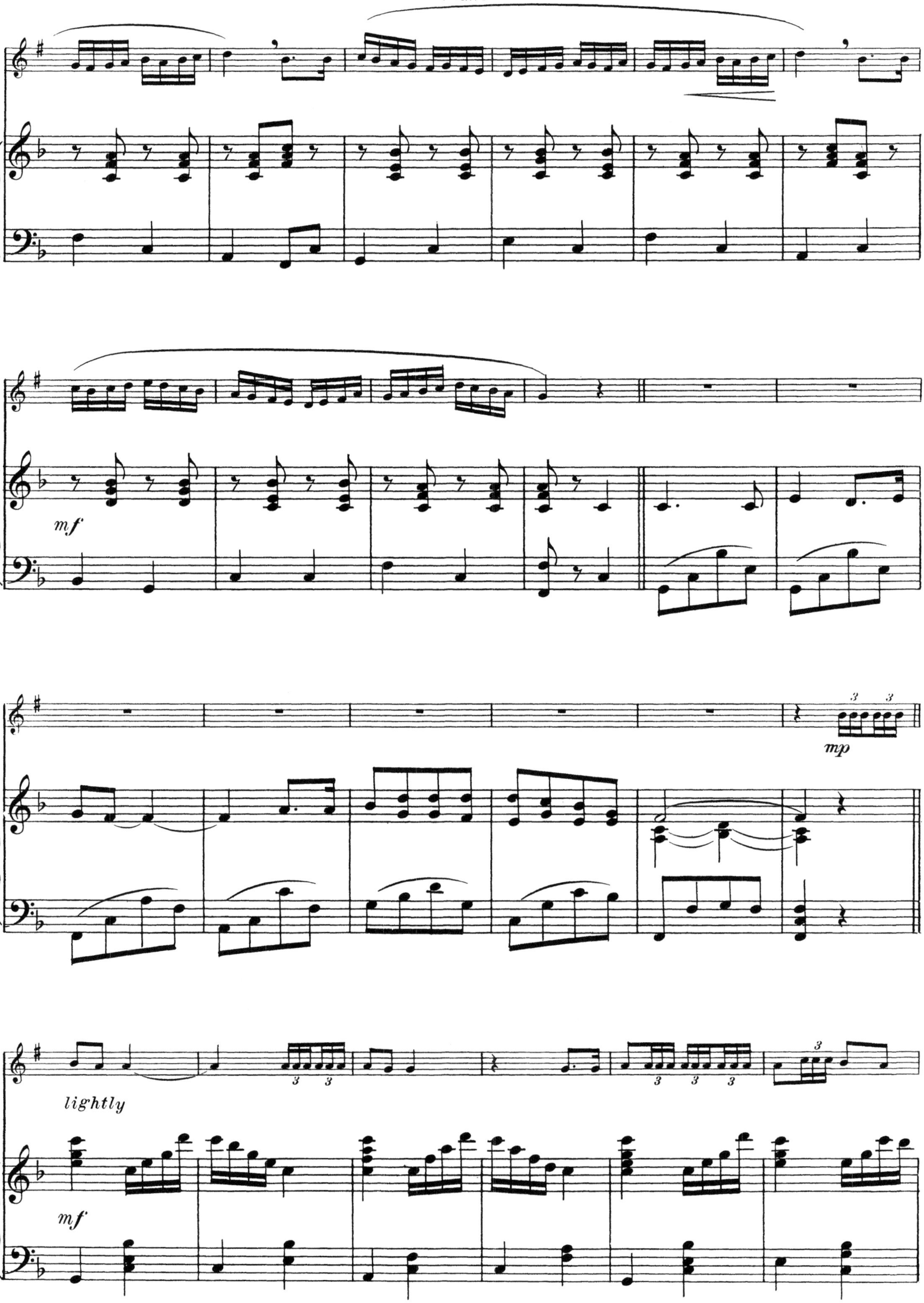
mf
mp
lightly
mf

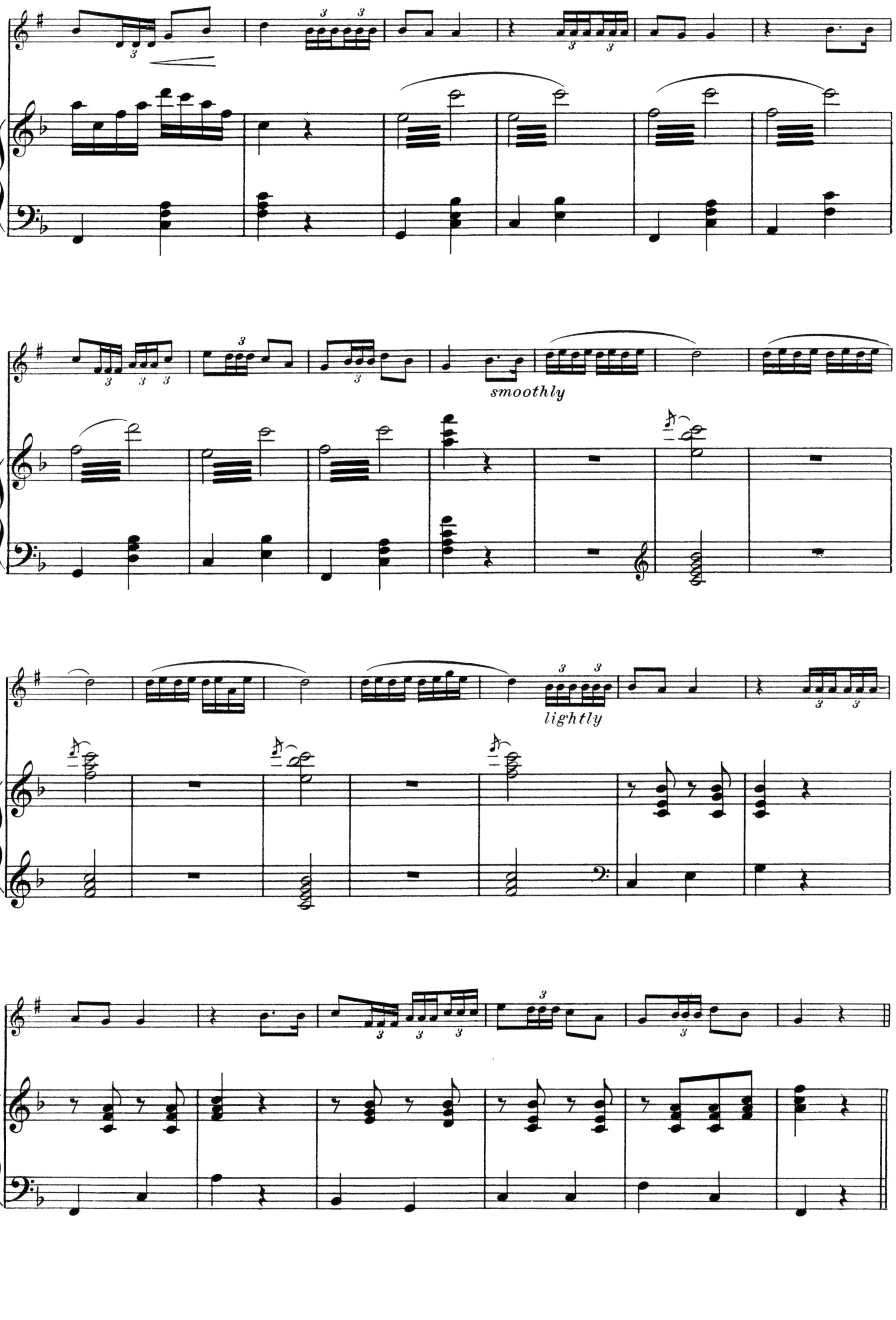
smoothly
lightly

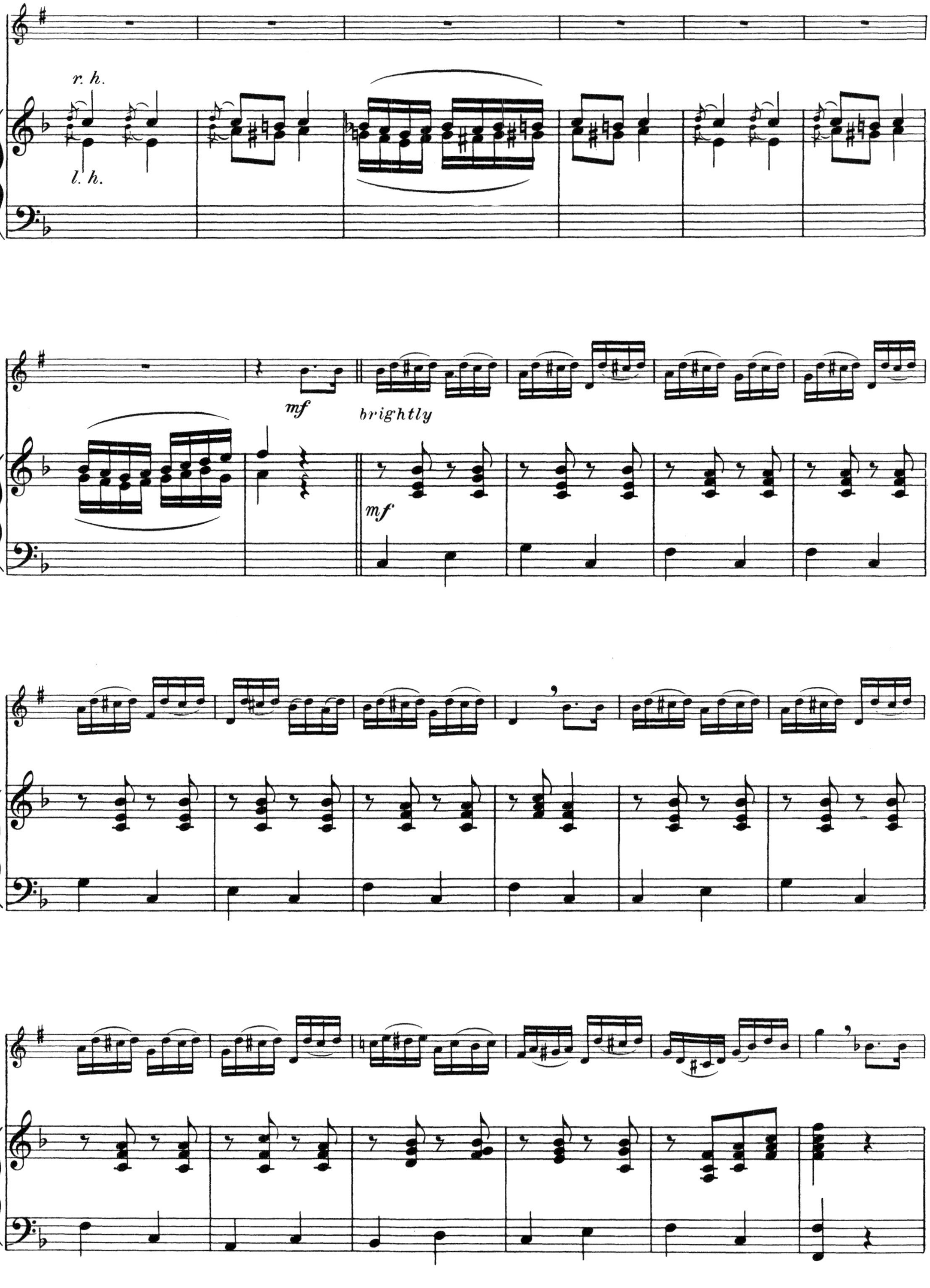
r. h.
l. h.
mf
brightly
mf

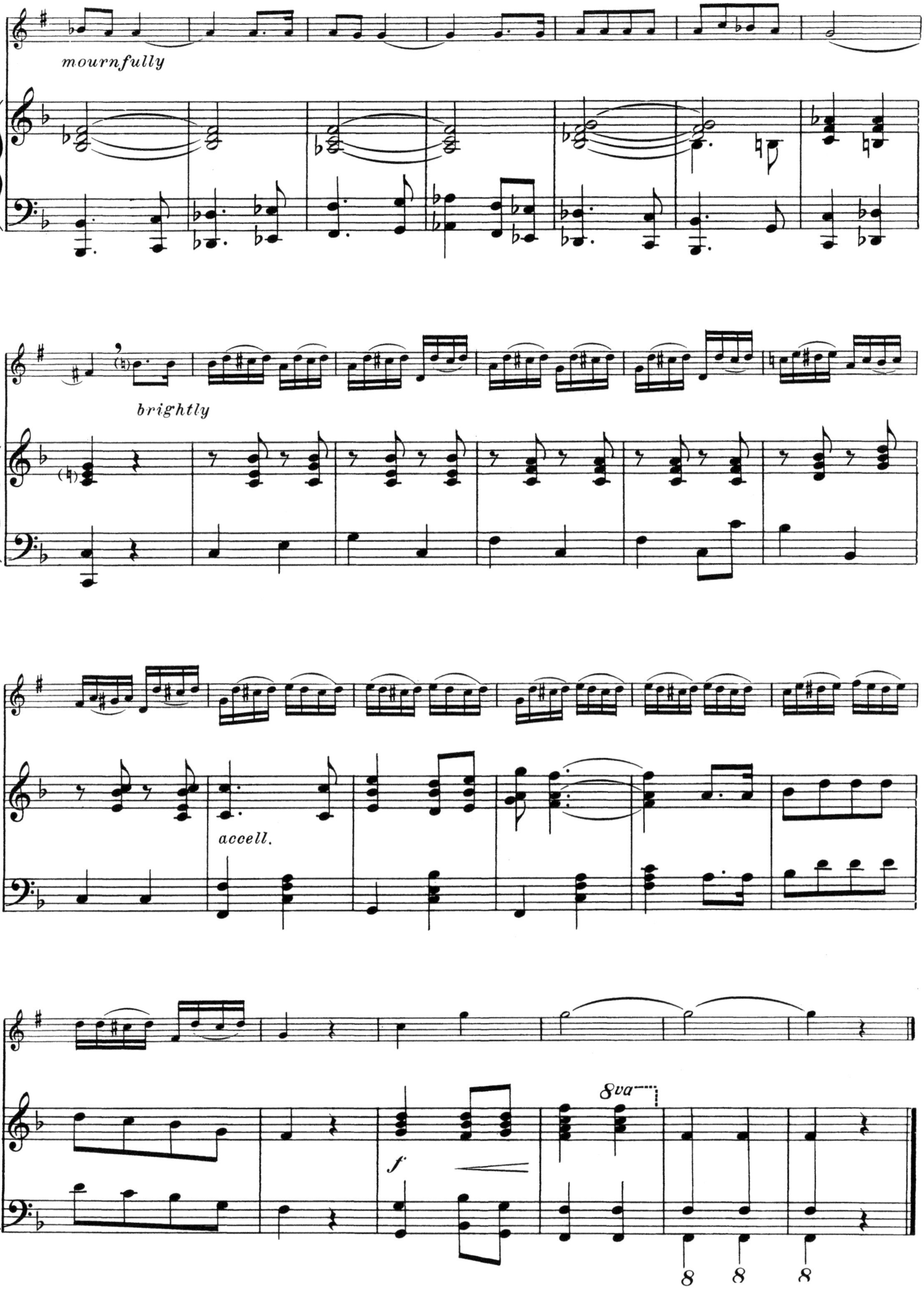
mournfully
brightly
accell.
f
8va

Adeste Fideles

(O Come, All Ye Faithful)

JOHN READING
Arr. by Henry W. Davis

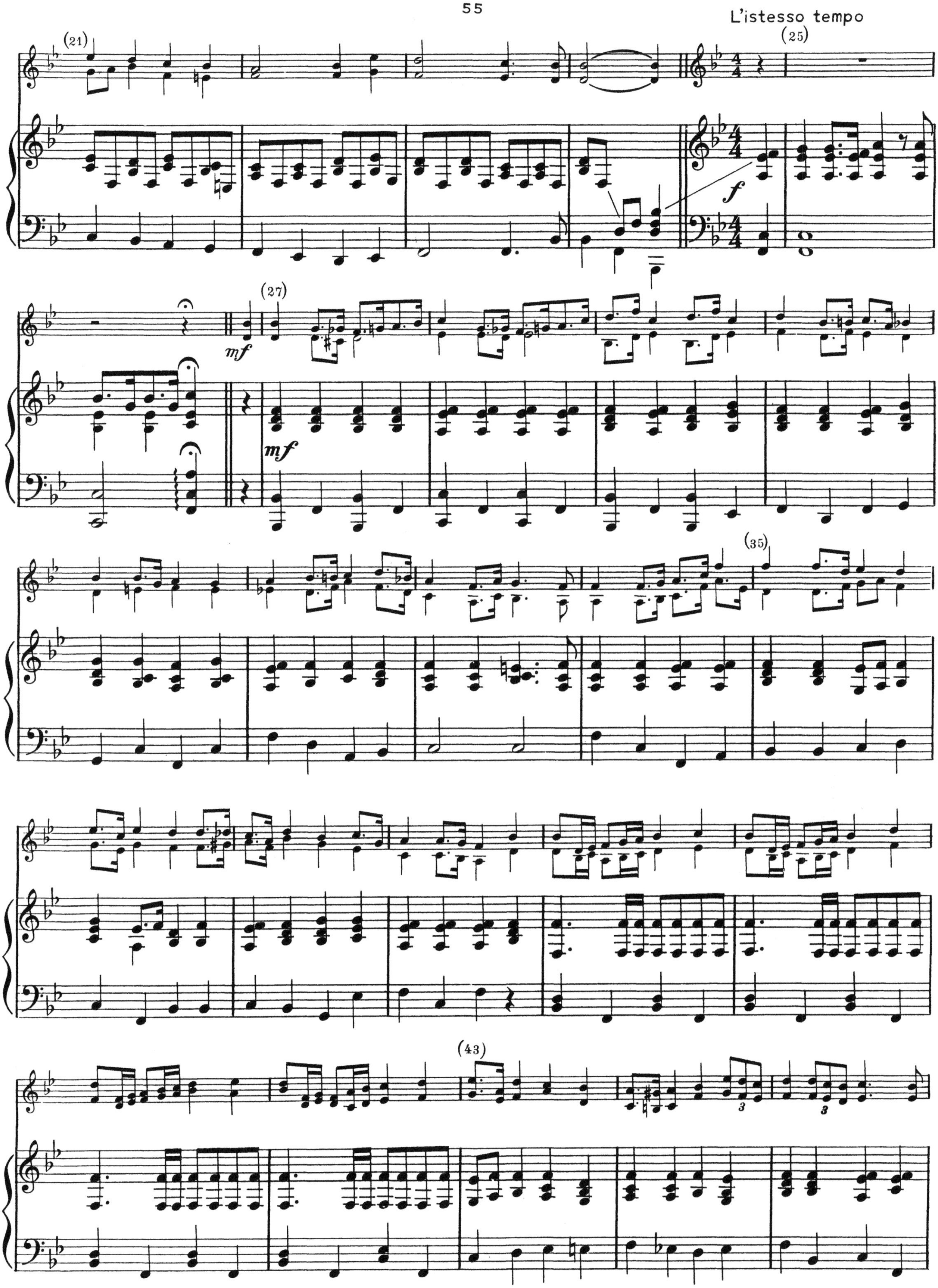
L'istesso tempo
(21)
(25)
(27)
mf
f
(35)
(43)

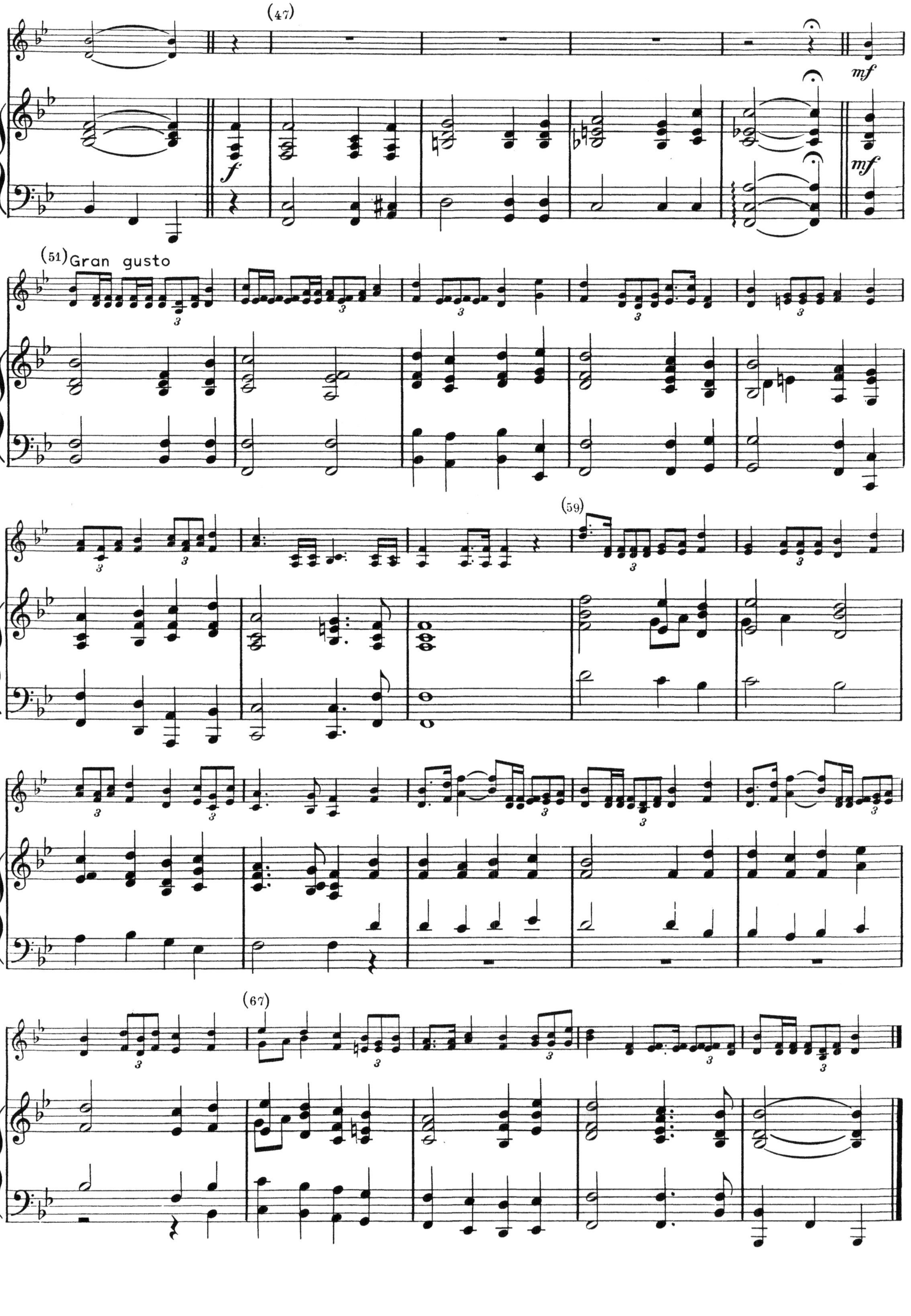
(47)
mf
f
mf
(51) Gran gusto
(59)
(67)